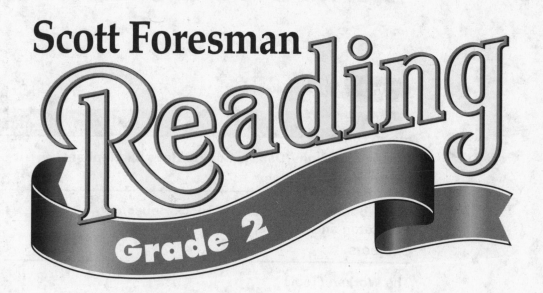

Scott Foresman
Reading
Grade 2

Grammar
Practice Book

Scott Foresman

Editorial Offices: Glenview, Illinois • Parsippany, New Jersey • New York, New York
Sales Offices: Reading, Massachusetts • Duluth, Georgia • Glenview, Illinois
Carrollton, Texas • Ontario, California

ISBN 0-328-00665-3

20 21 22 23 24 25 -DBH- 09 08 07

Table of Contents

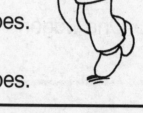

The kite   This is not a sentence.
             It does not tell what the kite does.
The kite flies high. This is a sentence.
                It tells what the kite does.

A **sentence** is a group of words that tells a complete idea.

Underline each group of words that is a sentence.

1. **a.** The wind blows.   2. **a.** Two girls fly kites.

   b. The wind   **b.** Two girls

3. **a.** One boy   4. **a.** Did a string break?

   b. One boy runs.   **b.** A string

5. **a.** His kite   6. **a.** One kite

   b. Does his kite go up?   **b.** One kite falls.

7. **a.** The kite flies far.   8. **a.** The girls

   b. The kite   **b.** The girls try again.

9. **a.** The boy   10. **a.** The children have fun.

   b. The boy holds on tight.   **b.** The children

Notes for Home: Your child identified complete sentences. **Home Activity:** Say a sentence to your child, such as *Bob went to the park*. Ask your child whether it is a sentence or not. Do the same with an incomplete sentence, such as *The tree*.

Circle each group of words that is a sentence.

1. Horses pull the wagons.
2. The race
3. Are the teams fast?
4. One wagon

5. Two dogs bark.
6. The people cheer.
7. The driver yells.
8. Our team wins.

Write each sentence you circled.

9. _____

10. _____

11. _____

12. _____

13. _____

14. _____

Notes for Home: Your child identified and wrote complete sentences. *Home Activity:* Write several sentences on strips of paper with your child. Cut the sentences in half, mix the papers, and have your child recombine them into sentences.

Name _____

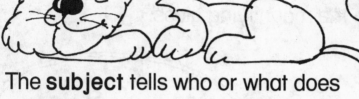

The **subject** tells who or what does something.

A lion sleeps by the tree.   **The baby** plays with the tail.

Circle the subject of each sentence.

1. The puppy brings the toy.   2. A squirrel runs up a tree.

3. The kitten rolls the ball.   4. A fox hides in a bush.

5. Birds sit on the branch.

Choose a simple subject for each sentence. **Write** it on the line.

6. The _____ crawls to a rock.

7. The _____ swims in the pond.

8. A _____ hops into the water.

9. A _____ lands on a flower.

10. A _____ makes a big splash.

duck
beaver
frog
turtle
bee

Notes for Home: Your child identified subjects as the parts of sentences that tell who or what does something. *Home Activity:* Ask your child questions about his or her classmates and what they do. Have your child identify the subjects in his or her responses.

Name _____

Find the subject to complete each sentence.
Use the subjects listed in the magnifying glass.

Sam and George
Fingerprints
The cookie thieves
The cookie jar
Alex

1. _____ is missing!

2. _____ are missing too.

3. _____ will collect everyone's fingerprints.

4. _____ are never the same.

5. _____ will be found!

Notes for Home: Your child added subjects to sentences. *Home Activity:* Help your child write sentences about family members. Remind your child that the subject of a sentence tells who or what does something.

4 Subjects

RETEACHING

The **predicate** tells what the subject is or does.

The girls **feed the fish.**

The fish **eat the food.**

Circle the predicate in each sentence.

1. Yesterday Sam called a friend.
2. His friend came over.
3. They played three games.
4. The friend went home.
5. Sam ate dinner.

Choose a predicate from the box for each sentence.
Write it on the line.

go to the lake.
swims with us.
fly in the sky.
is warm and still.

6. We _____

7. The water _____

8. Mom _____

9. The birds _____

Notes for Home: Your child identified and wrote predicates in sentences. ***Home Activity:***
Write two sentences. Have your child underline the predicate in each sentence. Then have
your child write two new sentences, using the same predicates.

Name _____

Draw a line from each subject to the predicate that matches it.

1. The fall   is a pretty time of year.

2. Many colorful leaves   rakes the leaves.

3. My brother   hide nuts in trees.

4. Sarah and I   jump in the leaves.

5. Some squirrels   are on the ground.

_____

Write a predicate to finish each sentence.

6. My friends and I _____

_____

_____ .

7. At school we _____

_____

_____ .

Notes for Home: Your child identified and wrote predicates in sentences. *Home Activity:* Write three sentences, and cut the paper between the subject and predicate. Have your child put the sentences back together correctly.

Name _____

RETEACHING

One fish jumps.   Does the bear get the fish?

Begin a **statement** with a capital letter. End a statement with a . . Begin a **question** with a capital letter. End a question with a ? .

Underline each statement.
Circle each question.

1. The deer eats leaves.

2. Squirrels find nuts.

3. Do birds eat worms?

4. Can you see the horses run?

5. Do bees like flowers?

6. Mice chew grass.

7. Does the fox hunt?

8. A bear sleeps.

Underline the correct statement or question in each pair.

9. a. The owl calls.
   b. the owl calls

10. a. a rabbit hides
    b. Can a rabbit hide?

11. a. Do you hear the bird sing?
    b. the bird sings

12. a. The toad hops.
    b. the toad hops

Notes for Home: Your child identified statements and questions. *Home Activity:* Pick a room in your home and have your child ask questions about where things are in the room. Then ask your child questions about a different room.

Statements and Questions 7

Name _____

Write these sentences correctly.
Use a period or a question mark at the end.

is there a gorilla in my room

_____

- -

_____

i saw a shadow on the wall

_____

- -

_____

it was near my bed

_____

- -

_____

was it big

_____

- -

_____

it was bigger than my dad

_____

- -

_____

Notes for Home: Your child wrote statements and questions. *Home Activity:* Play a round robin question game with your child and others. Write a simple question and hand it to the next person. He or she will answer the question and write a new question.

8 Statements and Questions

RETEACHING

Look at those trees.   What a huge forest!

Look at those trees. is a command.
It tells someone to do something.
What a huge forest! is an exclamation.
It shows strong feeling.

A **command** gives an order.
It ends with a **.** .
An **exclamation** shows strong feeling.
It ends with a **!** .

Circle each command.
Underline each exclamation.

1. Put the hammer away.

2. Pick up the crayons.

3. How tired we are!

4. How lucky that we are ready now!

5. Clear the stage.

6. What a funny play this will be!

Notes for Home: Your child identified commands and exclamations. *Home Activity:* Write simple sentences on cards. Show each card to your child and help him or her to restate the sentence as either a command or an exclamation.

Use a period after each command.
Use an exclamation mark after each exclamation.

1. Walk to that ride _____

2. What a long line _____

3. Find a seat _____

4. Lock your seat belt _____

5. How high up we are _____

6. What a fun ride _____

Write each command and exclamation.
Use a capital letter and the correct end mark.

7. look for Aunt Meg

_____

_____

8. how far away she seems

_____

_____

9. wave to her

_____

_____

10. i'm so happy to see her

_____

_____

Notes for Home: Your child identified and wrote commands and exclamations. *Home Activity:* Together, look at pictures of friends and family members, or pictures from magazines. Have your child write one command and one exclamation about the pictures.

10 **Commands and Exclamations**

Name _____

RETEACHING

A **boy** rides a **bike** to his **house**.
He sees his **dog**.

The noun **boy** names a person.
The noun **house** names a place.
The noun **dog** names an animal.
The noun **bike** names a thing.

A **noun** names a person, place, animal, or thing.

Circle each noun. There may be more than one in each sentence.

1. My grandma is here.

2. Dad walks the dog.

3. My friend comes to my house.

4. My aunt calls on the telephone.

5. Mr. Jones cooks in his kitchen.

6. I play in my room.

7. Mom works in her office.

8. Grandpa works in the garden.

9. Dad shops at the store.

10. A bird sits by my window.

11. The cat licks her paw.

12. Our roof needs to be fixed.

Notes for Home: Your child identified nouns—words for people, places, animals, or things—in sentences. **Home Activity:** Read a story with your child and have him or her point out each noun on one page of the story.

© Scott Foresman 2

Name _____

Circle each noun that names a person or an animal.

1. My uncle lives by the sea.

2. Seagulls like to play in his yard.

3. My brother sits on the porch.

4. Sometimes my dog hides in the garage.

5. Our aunt shows us the flowers.

6. Neighbors bring food from the fair.

7. The family eats in the kitchen.

Circle each noun.
Write on each line a noun that names a place.

The father took the girl to the _____. Her friend

came too. There were many children swimming. A man pointed

to a boat and a whale in the _____. A woman

watched a baby. Some people walked to the _____.

Soon it was time to go to their _____.

Notes for Home: Your child identified nouns in sentences. *Home Activity:* Have your child write as many nouns as possible on cards. Then he or she can categorize them as people, places, animals, or things.

Name _____

Why does Brian go to Littletown?

Pepper gets a checkup from
Dr. Williams.

Proper nouns are special names for people, animals, things, and places. They begin with capital letters.
Titles for people begin with capital letters. Most titles end with a period.

Circle each proper noun that should begin with a capital letter.
Circle two proper nouns in each sentence.

  1. wayne crane lives in the state of maine.

  2. He got his dog, nick, in the city of brunswick.

  3. His sister pat has a cat called matt.

Write a title or titles from the box in each sentence.

Ms. Mr. Mrs. Miss Dr.

  4. Today a neighbor, _____ Ann Blatt, watches Matt.

  5. _____ and _____ Crane take sick Nick to

       _____ Moore.

  6. _____ Susan Ko works for _____ Moore.

Notes for Home: Your child identified and capitalized proper nouns and titles for people.
Home Activity: Have your child show you his or her work on this page. Ask your child why each proper noun is capitalized.

Circle each title and proper noun that should have a capital letter.

1. My team doctor on our basketball team is dr. john.

2. My teacher, mrs. romero, likes him too.

3. My neighbor, mr. roth, gave our team a pet dog.

4. Its name is miss sunflower.

Correct each title and proper noun and write it.

5. _____

6. _____

7. _____

8. _____

Write a proper noun that names someone you know.

9. your teacher _____

10. your friend _____

11. a pet _____

Notes for Home: Your child identified and wrote proper nouns. **Home Activity:** Talk with your child about friends and neighbors. Have your child write three of their names, using capital letters correctly.

Name _____

RETEACHING

goat + s = goats

Many nouns add **-s** or **-es** to mean more than one.

Add -s or -es to the noun in ( ).
Write it on the line.

1. We went to see (farm). _____

2. Our (teacher) came with us. _____

3. We rode (bus). _____

4. We saw the chicken (coop). _____

5. I liked the (horse) best. _____

6. I hope we go on more (trip). _____

7. I love to see the (animal). _____

 Notes for Home: Your child added -s or -es to nouns to make them plural. **Home Activity:** Have your child draw a picture of his or her room. Ask your child to label the objects in the picture, using singular or plural nouns.

© Scott Foresman 2

Name _____

Underline each noun that means more than one.

1. One girl took out her pens.

2. Another girl found some crayons.

3. The boys wanted to draw a picture too.

4. The friends drew a spaceship.

5. They also drew two planes.

6. The teacher hung up the pictures.

Read each sentence.
Write the correct noun from the box to complete each sentence.

car	color	train
cars	colors	trains

7. I drew a picture of a _____ .

8. It had five long _____ .

9. I used many different _____ .

 Notes for Home: Your child practiced using singular and plural nouns. *Home Activity:* Have your child count various objects in your home and create sentences about them. For example, *We have one refrigerator.*

© Scott Foresman 2

Name _____

RETEACHING

Some **nouns** change to a different word
to mean more than one.

One	More Than One
man	men
woman	women
child	children

One	More Than One
foot	feet
tooth	teeth
goose	geese
mouse	mice

Look at each picture.
Circle the correct word.

1. mouse   mice

2. tooth   teeth

3. foot   feet

4. goose   geese

Change each word in ( ) to mean more than one.
Write the word in the sentence.

5. Those (man) _____ work in a hospital.

6. The (child) _____ are in their beds.

7. The (woman) _____ are doctors.

Notes for Home: Your child identified irregular plural nouns—nouns that change spelling to
mean more than one. **Home Activity:** Have your child write a poem, using the following
words: *teeth, feet,* and *children.*

Irregular Plural Nouns **17**

Answer each clue to solve the puzzle.
Write the answers in the boxes.

Across

2. more than one man

4. more than one child

5. more than one foot

Down

1. more than one woman

2. more than one mouse

3. more than one goose

6. more than one tooth

Notes for Home: Your child practiced writing irregular plural nouns. ***Home Activity:*** Have your child make up a dialogue between two farmers about sheep, geese, and mice. Your child can write, record, or illustrate the dialogue.

© Scott Foresman 2

Name _____

The **flags of the tents** are blowing.
The **tents' flags** are blowing.
Kim holds **the hand of her mother.**
Kim holds **her mother's hand.**
The **'** shows that the flags belong to the tents. The **'s** shows
that the hand belongs to the mother.

Many nouns add **'s** or **'** to show ownership.

Match the groups of words that say the same thing in a
different way.

1. the face of the clown   **a.** the elephants' trunks

2. the teeth of the tiger   **b.** the clown's face

3. the trunks of the elephants   **c.** the tiger's teeth

Add **'s** or **'** to each noun in ( ).
Write the noun in the sentence.

4. A (clown) _____ nose is red.

5. A (lion) _____ roar is loud.

6. The (bears) _____ act was fun.

Notes for Home: Your child identified possessive nouns. *Home Activity:* Have your child
make two sets of cards, one with people's names and one with names of things. Have him or
her pick a card from each pile and write a sentence, using both words. *(This is Jerry's car.)*

Possessive Nouns **19**

Name _____

Read the story.

Use **'s** or **'** to write the underlined words in a different way.

The whistle of the train blew. I looked at the watch of my mother. I could not wait to get to the city. The windows of the stores were filled with beautiful things. The eyes of my sister opened wide. We could not see the tops of the buildings. At night we saw the lights of the city. We had a good time!

_____

1. _____

2. _____

3. _____

4. _____

5. _____

6. _____

Notes for Home: Your child wrote possessive nouns in sentences. *Home Activity:* Ask your child questions about various family members' belongings. For example, *What color is Grandma's car?* Make sure that he or she uses a possessive noun to answer.

20 Possessive Nouns

The children **skip** to the music.

The word **skip** is a verb.
It tells what the children do.

A word that can show action is a **verb.**

Find the verb in each sentence.
Then **write** the verb.

1. The girls dance well.

2. They spin around the room.

3. All the children look.

4. Now some boys sing.

5. Friends listen to the song.

6. They clap loudly.

Notes for Home: Your child identified verbs in sentences. *Home Activity:* Watch a television show with your child. Ask him or her to tell you sentences about what people are doing. Write the sentences. Have your child circle the verbs in the sentences.

Name _____

Underline the verb in each sentence.

1. We wash our hands.   4. You pass the food.

2. My sisters mix the rice.   5. We eat dinner.

3. Mom and Dad set the table.   6. Friends knock on the door.

Choose the correct word from the box.
Write it in the sentence.

| gives | go | laugh | tell | play | open | sing |

7. You _____ the door.

8. Our friends _____ a story.

9. We _____ at the joke.

10. We all _____ a song.

11. Then we _____ a game.

12. He _____ a gift.

13. Then our friends _____ home.

Notes for Home: Your child identified and wrote verbs in sentences. *Home Activity:* Without speaking, do an action which your child can identify and describe in a sentence. (For example: jump, write, read, wash)

22 Verbs

© Scott Foresman 2

Name _____

One dog **barks.**   Two dogs **bark.**

Add **-s** to a verb to tell what one person, animal, or thing does. Do **not** add **-s** to a verb that tells what two or more people, animals, or things do.

Choose a verb in ( ).
Write the verb on the line.

1. Two cats (meow/meows).   _____

2. One mouse (climb/climbs).   _____

3. Three dogs (run/runs).   _____

Choose the correct verb.
Write it in the sentence.

4. Three fish (swim/swims) _____.

5. A turtle (swim/swims) _____ fast.

Notes for Home: Your child wrote verbs which agree with the subjects of sentences. *Home Activity:* Read a story with your child and have him or her identify all the singular subjects and verbs on one page. Do the same with plural subjects and verbs.

Subject/Verb Agreement 23

Match each subject to the correct predicate.
Draw a line.

1. Spotted pigs   run very fast.

2. An old cow   kicks a pail.

3. Young horses   play in mud.

4. A brown rooster   sits on a fence.

Choose the correct verb from the box.
Write it on the line to finish each sentence.

| grow | grows | taste | tastes | work | works |

5. A farmer _____ in the field.

6. Farmers _____ hard.

7. They _____ corn.

8. A corn plant _____ tall.

9. The sweet corn _____ good.

Notes for Home: Your child matched subjects and verbs that agree in sentences. **Home Activity:** Say a subject. (For example: *The tiny insect*) Have your child finish the sentence by saying a verb that correctly matches the subject and adds more information.

© Scott Foresman 2

RETEACHING

Today Karen **shows** something.
Last week Bob **showed** something.
Next week Lou **will show** something.

The verb **shows** tells about now. It ends with **-s.**
The verb **showed** tells about the past. It ends with **-ed.**
The verb **will show** tells about the future. It begins with **will.**

Underline the verb in each sentence.
Then circle **Now** or **Past.**

1. Today Karen points to a hat.   Now   Past

2. Last time she showed us a trick box.   Now   Past

3. Then Karen explained the trick.   Now   Past

4. Now she turns the hat over.   Now   Past

5. Karen picks the next person.   Now   Past

Circle the correct verb in ( ) for each sentence.

6. Now Flora (looks/looked) into the hat.

7. Next week Bob (talked/will talk) about his dog.

8. Now Karen (pulls/pulled) out a picture.

9. She (shows/will show) the picture tomorrow too.

10. Last Monday Greg (learns/learned) a new game.

Notes for Home: Your child identified verbs in the present, past, and future tenses. *Home Activity:* Take a walk with your child and talk about what you see and hear. Help your child use verbs in the correct tenses.

© Scott Foresman 2

Name _____

Underline the correct verb in ( ) for each sentence.

1. Jessie says she (wants / wanted) to see a movie.

2. A few hours ago she (picks / picked) a show.

3. After that she (walks / walked) to town.

4. Now the movie (ends / ended).

5. Jessie (laughs / laughed) when the movie was over.

6. The same movie (will play / played) next week.

Add -s, -ed, or **will** to each word in the box.
Write the correct verb in each sentence.

| talk | ask | learn | explain |

7. Last night Jessie _____ about the movie.

8. Today Dad _____ questions.

9. Later Jessie _____ the story.

10. Jessie _____ the story well.

Notes for Home: Your child identified and wrote verbs in the present, past, and future tenses. *Home Activity:* Talk with your child about a family event. Help him or her use the present, past, and future tenses correctly.

26 Verb Tenses (Present, Past, and Future)

Name _____

RETEACHING

Today it **rains.**
Yesterday it **rained.**
Tomorrow it **will rain.**

Be sure to use the correct verb to show something happening now, in the past, or in the future.

Circle the verb in each sentence.
Then **write** the verb.

1. They stayed inside. _____

2. Jason plays a game. _____

3. Kim will watch TV. _____

4. Ann cleaned her room. _____

Underline the correct verb in ( ) for each sentence.

5. Yesterday Jason (paint / painted) a picture.

6. Tomorrow Kim (color / will color) with crayons.

7. Now the dog (jumps / jumped) on them.

Notes for Home: Your child identified and wrote verbs in the correct tenses in sentences.
Home Activity: Write a sentence on a piece of paper, leaving out the verb. *(Yesterday
we _____ a movie.)* Have your child write a verb in the correct tense.

Add -ed, -s, or **will** to the words in ( ).

1. An hour ago we (turn) _____ the lights off.

2. Soon Mike (walk) _____ into the room.

3. Then Barbara (yell) _____, "Surprise!"

4. Now she (hide) _____.

Complete each sentence with a verb from the box.

will open   play   thanked   laughed

5. Mike _____ at our trick.

6. Soon Mike _____ his presents.

7. He _____ everyone for the surprise.

8. Now we _____ the new games.

Notes for Home: Your child completed sentences by adding verbs in the correct tenses. **Home Activity:** Choose a verb and have your child write sentences, using that verb in the present, past, and future tenses.

© Scott Foresman 2

Name _____

Circle the word in ( ) that makes sense in each sentence.

We (are / is) going to school today.

Tomorrow I (was / will be) staying home.

The verbs **is, are, was, were,** and **will be** do not show action.
The verbs **is** and **are** tell about now.
The verbs **was** and **were** tell about the past.
The verb **will be** tells about the future.

Draw lines to connect sentence parts and make sentences.

1. The sun	is cool.	
2. Boats	is bright.	
3. The lake	are ready.	
4. The races	are today.	

5. The sky	are up.	
6. The sails	is clear.	
7. Dina	is busy.	

Underline the correct word in ( ) for each sentence.

8. The show (was / were) exciting.

9. Many people (was / were) there.

10. It (was / were) lots of fun.

Write a sentence using **will be.**

_____

- -

_____

- -

Notes for Home: Your child wrote forms of the verb *to be*, such as *is, was, are, were,* and *will be,* in sentences. ***Home Activity:*** Talk with your child about what he or she did last year that is different from this year. Remind your child to use the correct forms of the verb *to be*.

Write **is, are, was, were,** or **will be** to complete each sentence correctly.

1. Dad and I _____ hiking for hours this morning.

2. When we got there, Lost Lake _____ very crowded.

3. Now Dad _____ looking for a different lake.

4. He said, "We _____ not going to camp with the crowd."

5. We _____ cold and wet when we set up the tent.

6. I _____ so happy when we go back home!

Notes for Home: Your child completed sentences by adding forms of the verb *to be (is, are, was, were, will be)*. **Home Activity:** Write *is, are, was, were,* and *will be* on cards. Have your child choose a card and write a sentence with that form of the verb *to be.*

RETEACHING

Words for number, size, and shape are **adjectives**.

Ten leaves fall.   The tree has **large** leaves.
The leaves have **pointed** edges.

Underline the adjective for number, size, or shape in each sentence.

1. The round leaves are gone.

2. The boy puts leaves in two piles.

3. The children collect big leaves.

4. A small squirrel climbs on the tree.

Circle the adjective for number, size, or shape in each sentence.
Write the adjective on the line.

5. The squirrel looks for large nuts.   _____

6. Its round ears hear the children.   _____

7. Two girls smile at the squirrel.   _____

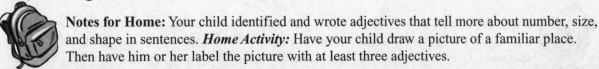

Notes for Home: Your child identified and wrote adjectives that tell more about number, size, and shape in sentences. **Home Activity:** Have your child draw a picture of a familiar place. Then have him or her label the picture with at least three adjectives.

Name _____

Write the adjective in ( ) on the line.

1. Chris wears a _____ hat in the school play.
   (shoe/big)

2. Kara is the girl in the _____ coat.
   (small/slowly)

3. They have _____ parrots.
   (three/fly)

Complete each sentence with an adjective from the box.

tall	little	two	square

4. Kara looks at the _____ parrots.

5. The parrots hide in a _____ tree.

6. Kara puts the parrots in _____ cages.

7. The cages have _____ doors.

Notes for Home: Your child identified and wrote adjectives that tell more about size, shape, and number in sentences. *Home Activity:* Have your child write sentences about family members. Challenge him or her to use at least one adjective in each sentence.

Name _____

RETEACHING

An **adjective** describes a person, place, animal, or thing.

An adjective can tell how something looks, sounds, tastes, feels, or smells.

The cake tastes **sweet.**

Circle the adjective in each sentence.
Draw a line from each adjective to the sense it matches.

1. Our kittens feel soft.

2. My soup tastes spicy.

3. The trees look green.

4. The air smells fresh.

5. The drum sounds loud.

6.

7.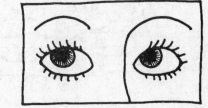

8.

9.

10.

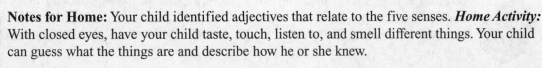

Notes for Home: Your child identified adjectives that relate to the five senses. ***Home Activity:*** With closed eyes, have your child taste, touch, listen to, and smell different things. Your child can guess what the things are and describe how he or she knew.

Name _____

Choose an adjective from the box that makes sense in each sentence.

Write it on the line.

hot   sweet   wet   rotten   loud

1. My sister's voice is _____.

2. The apples feel _____ in the water.

3. Be careful of the _____ tea on the stove!

4. There is a bad apple that smells _____.

5. Our apple pies will taste _____.

Notes for Home: Your child identified adjectives that describe sight, sound, taste, feel, and smell. **Home Activity:** Have your child choose things that he or she sees, hears, tastes, feels, and smells. Your child can write each thing on one side of a card and list adjectives on the other side.

RETEACHING

The kitten plays.   The **fuzzy** kitten plays.
The word **kitten** is a noun.
The adjective **fuzzy** tells more about the noun **kitten.**

An **adjective** describes a person, place, animal, or thing.

The word in ( ) is an adjective. It tells more about the noun.
Write the word in the sentence. **Read** the complete sentence.

1. Pedro pulls the _____ string. (long)

2. The _____ mouse moves. (brown)

3. The kitten chases the _____ toy. (little)

4. The toy goes under the _____ chair. (big)

5. The _____ kitten meows. (sad)

6. Now Pedro and the kitten play with a _____ ball. (blue)

Notes for Home: Your child wrote adjectives—words that describe—in sentences. *Home Activity:* Have your child look at pictures in magazines. Then have him or her write two sentences about the pictures, using at least one adjective in each sentence.

Writing with Adjectives **35**

Draw one line under the adjective in each sentence.
Draw two lines under the noun it tells more about.

1. The silly movie starts.

2. The happy children sit.

3. Then fast music begins.

4. A gray donkey runs.

5. A tiny donkey trots.

6. They step on a large hat.

7. A tall cowboy comes.

8. Is he a brave man?

Choose the better adjective in ( ) to tell more about the noun.
Write the adjective in the sentence.

9. The _____ thunder crashes. (loud / quiet)

10. The _____ cattle run away. (safe / scared)

11. The cowboy calls the _____ donkey. (pink / gray)

12. The donkey chases the _____ cattle. (wild / dry)

13. The cattle sleep in the _____ barn. (tiny / big)

14. The _____ cowboy goes home. (tired / new)

Notes for Home: Your child identified and wrote adjectives—words that tell more about nouns—in sentences. **Home Activity:** Have your child draw an imaginary creature. Then help him or her write a short story about the creature, using at least four adjectives.

Name _____

RETEACHING

small   smaller   smallest

Add **-er** to an adjective to compare two persons, places, or things.

Add **-est** to an adjective to compare three or more persons, places, or things.

Add -er to each word.
Write the new word.

1. old

2. hard

3. cool

_____

- - - - - - - - - - - -

_____

Add -est to the word in ( ).
Write the new word in the sentence.

4. Our school has the (loud) _____ band.

5. The bells make the (soft) _____ music.

6. We play the (long) _____ song last.

Notes for Home: Your child wrote comparative and superlative adjectives in sentences. *Home Activity:* Have your child choose three objects in your home *(shoes, glasses, pictures)* and use comparative and superlative adjectives to compare the objects.

© Scott Foresman 2

Comparative and Superlative Adjectives **37**

Circle a word in ( ) to complete the sentence.
Think first if two or more things are compared.

1. This car is (slower / slowest) than that car.

2. The seats are (higher / highest) than those in Jo's car.

3. Abe is the (younger / youngest) driver on the street.

4. This road is the (longer / longest) one in town.

5. That kitten is the (smaller / smallest) one in the litter.

Add -er or **-est** to each word in ( ).
Write the new word in the sentence.

6. A car is (small) _____ than a bus.

7. A train is (long) _____ than a bus.

8. This jet is the (fast) _____ of all the
planes.

9. That is the (old) _____ ship I have seen.

10. My father is (tall) _____ than his brother.

Notes for Home: Your child wrote comparative and superlative adjectives. *Home Activity:*
Have your child compare family members. Remind them to use comparative and superlative
adjectives.

© Scott Foresman 2

RETEACHING

The music plays **now**.   The children walk **around**.
The children laughed **loudly**.

An adverb can tell **when, where,** or **how**.
The word **now** tells **when** the music plays.
The word **around** tells **where** the children walk.
The word **loudly** tells **how** the children laugh.

An **adverb** can tell more about a verb.

Circle the adverb that tells about each underlined verb.

1. The children play inside.   4. The players sit now.

2. The chairs stand there.   5. Two children stand up.

3. The music stops quickly.   6. A boy takes a chair carefully.

Underline When if the circled adverb tells when. **Underline Where** if the circled adverb tells where. **Underline How** if the circled adverb tells how.

7. The game ends (soon)   **When   Where   How**

8. The children go (outside)   **When   Where   How**

9. They walk (slowly)   **When   Where   How**

10. (Then) the teacher calls them.   **When   Where   How**

Notes for Home: Your child identified and wrote adverbs in sentences. *Home Activity:* Have your child draw a picture of himself or herself doing something at school. Then have your child write sentences about the drawing, using at least one adverb.

Complete each sentence with an adverb from one of these lists.

When	**Where**	**How**
then	up	carefully
today	inside	quickly
soon	outside	quietly
now	down	loudly

I. Our class visited a museum _____.

2. We drove there _____ in a school bus.

3. First, we saw a plant exhibit _____.

4. Then, we walked _____ the museum.

5. We looked _____ at huge dinosaur skeletons.

Notes for Home: Your child wrote adverbs in sentences. *Home Activity:* Read a favorite story with your child. Have him or her point out three adverbs. Then have him or her write new sentences, using the adverbs.

Name _____

RETEACHING

Mrs. Catalano is an art teacher.
She is an art teacher.

The word **she** is a pronoun.
It takes the place of the noun **Mrs. Catalano.**

A **pronoun** is a word that takes the place of a noun or nouns.
The words **he, she, it, we,** and **they** are pronouns.

Draw a line under the pronoun in each sentence.

1. We saw a movie in art class.

2. It was about a man in New Mexico.

3. He made sand paintings for a friend.

4. She loved the colors of the sand.

5. They were beautiful.

6. Our art teacher says we can make sand paintings.

7. She is going to show the class how.

Write the pronoun that can take the place of the noun. Use **he, she, we,** and **they.**

8. James Wolf _____

9. Ed and Flo _____

10. Ms. Silverwater _____

11. Jack and I _____

Notes for Home: Your child identified and wrote pronouns in sentences. *Home Activity:* Say sentences about people your child knows. *(Mr. and Mrs. Jones have a garden.)* Have your child replace the people's names with pronouns. *(They have a garden.)*

Name _____

Circle the pronoun you can use in place of the word or words in ( ).

1. (Mrs. Choy) saves old newspapers.   He   She

2. (The papers) are in the garage.   They   It

3. (Dennis and I) put the papers in a car.   We   They

4. (Dennis) drives the car.   She   He

5. (The car) is filled with newspapers!   It   We

Write **he, she, it, we,** and **they** in the letter. One of the pronouns will be used twice.

Dear Alex,

     I collect empty cans. _____ have to be cleaned. Then

_____ take the cans to a special place. _____ makes

the cans useful again. _____ will be used for many

things. My brother said _____ will save cans too. Ask your

mom if your family can help. I hope _____ says yes.

Your friend,

Eva

 Notes for Home: Your child identified and wrote pronouns in sentences. ***Home Activity:*** Write the pronouns *he, she, we, it,* and *they* on cards. Have your child choose a card and say a sentence, using that pronoun.

42 Pronouns

He, she, and **it** are pronouns that name only one.
We and **they** are pronouns that name more than one.

He holds the bag.
They clean the yard.

Read the sentences.
Circle the pronoun that can take the place of the underlined word or words.

1. <u>Jason and his friends</u> go to a birthday party. (They / She) bring presents.

2. The birthday party is for <u>Heather</u>. (It / She) is seven years old.

3. <u>The party</u> started at noon. (It / They) will end at three o'clock.

4. <u>Jason</u> loves birthday cake. (We / He) asks if it is a chocolate cake.

5. <u>Heather and I</u> tell Jason that the cake is chocolate. (They / We) laugh when he smiles.

6. We eat the whole <u>cake</u>, and we tell our parents that (she / it) was good.

Notes for Home: Your child matched noun phrases to singular and plural pronouns *(he, she, it, we, they)*. **Home Activity:** Together, make flashcards with sentences about friends, family, and your child. Help your child underline subjects and write pronouns on the other side of the cards.

Name _____

Circle each pronoun that means one person or thing.
Underline each pronoun that means more than one.

I. he **2.** she **3.** we **4.** they **5.** it

Choose a pronoun from the box to take the place of each
underlined word or group of words.
Write it on the line.

He	She	They	It	We

6. <u>Richard</u> is crying. _____

7. <u>Her bugle</u> is new. _____

8. <u>Sheri and Dan</u> are blowing

up balloons. _____

9. <u>Mom and I</u> made a big sandwich.
_____

10. <u>My sister</u> wakes up early. _____

Notes for Home: Your child identified and used singular and plural pronouns in sentences.
Home Activity: Have your child tell you about a movie or TV show he or she has seen. Help
your child recognize the pronouns he or she uses.

RETEACHING

The pronouns **I, he, she, we,** and **they** are used as subjects of sentences.
The pronouns **me, him, her, us,** and **them** are used after action verbs.
The pronouns **you** and **it** can be used anywhere in a sentence.

Draw a line from the underlined word or group of words to the pronoun that can take its place.

I. <u>My grandmother and I</u> are sitting on the couch.   him

2. <u>My grandmother</u> is telling me about her friend, Bob.   We

3. Grandmother saw <u>Bob</u> at a party.   them

4. <u>Bob's children</u> were at the party too.   She

5. Grandmother gave <u>Bob's children</u> some cake.   They

Notes for Home: This week your child reviewed pronouns used in subjects and predicates of sentences. **Home Activity:** Ask your child to read a story to you. Have your child keep a tally of the number of pronouns used as subjects and the number of pronouns used in predicates.

© Scott Foresman 2

Subject and Object Pronouns **45**

Name _____

Find the word that best fits in each sentence.
Mark the space for your answer.

1. _____ love to play music!

   ⊂◯ She   ⊂◯ Us   ⊂◯ We

2. Susie brought drums and played _____ .

   ⊂◯ they   ⊂◯ her   ⊂◯ them

3. Herbie's piano is loud. He plays a special song on _____.

   ⊂◯ us   ⊂◯ it   ⊂◯ she

4. Where did _____ learn to play the guitar?

   ⊂◯ them   ⊂◯ him   ⊂◯ he

5. The audience is clapping for _____!

   ⊂◯ we   ⊂◯ I   ⊂◯ us

6. We are glad _____ came to listen.

   ⊂◯ they   ⊂◯ her   ⊂◯ us

© Scott Foresman 2

Notes for Home: Your child chose the best subject or object pronoun to fit in a sentence. *Home Activity:* Have your child write *I, she, he, we, they, you, me, her, him, us, them,* and *it* on cards. Pick one of the cards and ask your child a question using the word on the card.

A **pronoun** takes the place of a noun or nouns.
When you use pronouns, you don't need to
use the same noun over and over.

Joe likes **cats**. **He** plays with **them**.

Read each sentence.
Choose a pronoun from the box to finish the second sentence in each pair. **Write** it on the line.
Circle the word or words in the first sentence in each pair that helped you decide which pronoun to use.

He	She	It	them	They

I. A woman came to visit our class.

_____ was from Guinea.

2. Guinea is a country in West Africa.

_____ is on the coast of the Atlantic Ocean.

3. The woman and her brother told us about their country.

_____ spoke to us in English.

4. They showed us clothes from Guinea.

They even let us try _____ on!

Notes for Home: Your child replaced nouns and noun phrases with pronouns in sentences.
Home Activity: Have your child pretend he or she is visiting another country. Ask him or her to write a postcard to you from the other country, using several pronouns.

Read each sentence and question.
Answer each question by writing a pronoun from the box on the line.

she	it	them	her	he	us	we	they

1. Sally has a messy room. What should Sally do?

   _____   _____

   _____ should clean _____.

2. There are toys everywhere. What should Sally do with the toys?

   _____   _____

   _____ should put _____ away.

3. Sally can't find her homework. What should Sally do?

   _____   _____

   _____ should look for _____.

4. John wants to help Sally. What should John do?

   _____   _____

   _____ should start helping _____.

5. John and Sally finished cleaning. What should John and Sally do?

   _____

   _____ should have lunch!

Notes for Home: Your child used pronouns in sentences. **Home Activity:** Encourage your child to use pronouns to write about a day he or she really enjoyed.

© Scott Foresman 2

RETEACHING

Roy **is not** late. Roy **isn't** late.
Isn't is a short way to write **is** and **not**.
An apostrophe **'** takes the place of **o** in **not**.

A contraction is a short way to put two words together. An apostrophe **'** takes the place of one or more letters.

Circle the contraction for the underlined words.

1. The people <u>are not</u> ready.   aren't   didn't

2. They <u>have not</u> found a seat.   haven't   wouldn't

3. The train <u>should not</u> leave.   isn't   shouldn't

4. The train <u>does not</u> go yet.   doesn't   don't

5. The people <u>would not</u> be safe.   couldn't   wouldn't

Circle the words that make up the underlined contraction.

6. <u>She's</u> here to help.   She is   She will

7. Now they<u>'ll</u> sit down.   you will   they will

8. Then <u>we'll</u> hear the whistle.   we will   we are

9. At last <u>we're</u> on our way.   they are   we are

Notes for Home: Your child identified contractions correctly in sentences. *Home Activity:* Write contractions, such as *isn't, doesn't,* or *we're,* on cards. Choose a card and have your child use that contraction in a sentence. Then change roles.

Name _____

Write the contraction for each set of words in ( ).

| He's | don't | doesn't | isn't |

1. The kittens (do not) _____ move.

2. Jon (does not) _____ see them.

3. (He is) _____ going by the chair.

4. The chair (is not) _____ empty.

Write the words for the contractions in ( ).

| We are | We will | They will | They are |

5. (They're) _____ jumping out.

6. (We're) _____ laughing at the kittens.

7. (They'll) _____ make us laugh every time.

8. (We'll) _____ play with them again tomorrow.

Notes for Home: Your child wrote contractions in sentences. **Home Activity:** Write a sentence on a piece of paper. (For example: *We are going now.*) Have your child rewrite the sentence, using a contraction. *(We're going now.)*

Name _____

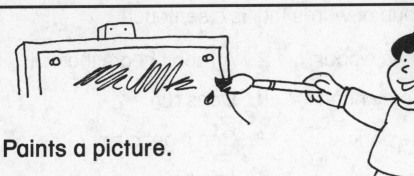

Paints a picture.

This group of words is not a sentence.
It does not tell a complete idea.

Luis paints a picture.

This group of words is a sentence. It tells a complete idea.

Underline each group of words that is a sentence.

1. a. Lin draws people.

   b. Draws people.

2. a. Need a pencil?

   b. Does he need a pencil?

3. a. Nan clay.

   b. Nan works with clay.

4. a. She makes a cup.

   b. Makes a cup.

Draw a line to match each group of words with the correct sentence.

5. Bring crayons?

6. Mimi found.

7. I brought.

8. Made a sign.

a. I brought some paper.

b. Did Sam bring crayons?

c. Mimi found the tape.

d. We made a sign.

Notes for Home: Your child identified complete sentences. *Home Activity:* Have your child draw a picture and write an advertisement for a favorite food. Remind your child to use complete sentences.

© Scott Foresman 2

Complete Sentences 51

Underline each group of words that is a sentence.

1. Animals live in the woods.

2. A rabbit hears the call.

3. Some animals may hunt.

4. Does run.

5. They hunt in the dark.

6. Can it get away?

7. Runs at night.

8. In a hole.

9. Howls at the moon.

10. Rabbit is.

11. A rabbit.

12. Will the rabbit sleep?

Now **write** the other groups of words in complete sentences.

13. _____

14. _____

15. _____

16. _____

17. _____

18. _____

Notes for Home: Your child wrote complete sentences. **Home Activity:** Together, write a sentence. Cut the paper between the subject and predicate. *(The rabbit/hopped away.)* Have your child write two new sentences, using the subject in one and the predicate in another.

© Scott Foresman 2

Name _____

RETEACHING

Quotation marks show the beginning and ending of what someone says.

"How much is this?" asked Nancy.

The saleswoman said, "It is one dollar."

Finish each sentence.
Remember to put quotation marks around what someone says.

1. The baker said, _____

_____

_____

2. _____

_____

_____ asked Billy.

3. My friend said, _____

_____

_____

4. _____

_____ yelled the boy to his dog.

Notes for Home: Your child used quotation marks to show a speaker's exact words in sentences. **Home Activity:** Have your child tell you about a conversation he or she had. Write it, leaving out the quotation marks. Have your child insert quotation marks.

© Scott Foresman 2

Name _____

Add quotation marks if the sentence needs them.
Write an **X** next to the sentences that don't need quotation marks.

1. Where should we go to dinner tonight? asked Mom.

2. The children looked at each other with big smiles.

3. Let's go to the pizza place! they yelled.

Read the sentences.
Cross out the quotation marks that do not belong.

"Did you make this sandcastle?" asked my friend.**X**

4.–10.

"Do you want to make a treehouse?"
Joey asked his friends.
"Yes! Great idea!" his friends
answered."
Joey said, "I'll get the hammer and"
nails."
"What should we get?" asked" his friends.
"Get some wood," said Joey. Joey
found the hammer and nails, and his
friends found some wood. "Joey and
his friends built a great treehouse."

Notes for Home: Your child made decisions about where quotation marks belong in
sentences. **Home Activity:** Have your child look through a newspaper and find sentences with
quotation marks.

54 Quotation Marks

© Scott Foresman 2

Commas are used in addresses:

6000 Michigan Avenue, Apt. 3
Chicago, IL 60615

Commas are used in dates: March 15, 2001

Commas are used to start letters: Dear Marge,

Commas are used to separate three or more things:
I need to buy rice, sugar, and milk.

Commas are used to end a letter: Your friend,
Jimmy

Add commas where they belong in this letter.

1.–8.

Jake Fountain
321 Miller Court Apt. 6A
Boulder CO 83009

July 6 2001

Dear Dad
Summer camp is great! Today we went hiking
swimming and biking. Tomorrow we will cook
hamburgers hot dogs fries and sweet corn.

Love
Tabitha

Notes for Home: Your child inserted commas into the following parts of a letter: the address,
the date, the greeting, items in a series, and the closing. **Home Activity:** Have your child write
a letter to you about something funny that happened at school.

Name _____

Read this letter.

44 Dixie Lane
New Orleans, LA 70003
June 3, 2000

Dear Friend,

Hi. I just moved into this neighborhood. I come from Lincoln, Nebraska. I have a cat, a dog, and a bird. I was wondering if you would like to come over for lunch on Saturday, June 10.

Sincerely,
Mindy

Write a letter in response to the letter above.
Remember to use commas.

_____

_____

_____

_____

_____

_____

Notes for Home: Your child read and wrote letters with commas. *Home Activity:* Write a letter to your child, and have him or her circle the commas and then write back to you.

56 Commas

© Scott Foresman 2

A **comma** is placed between the date and the year.

A **comma** is also placed between the day of the week and the date.

Priscilla will be seven years old on May 5, 2003.
We're going to Miami on Sunday, April 19.

Commas are also used to join two complete sentences with a connecting word, such as *and*.

I like to swim, and my brother likes to hike.

1.–4. Circle the commas in this paragraph.

Max's sister is the smartest girl in the school. She is graduating on June 22, 2002. She will read a speech to her classmates, and they will all sing a song. Max can bring one friend to her party on Monday, June 23. Max is going to buy his sister a book, and he is going to give her a card.

Add commas where they belong.

5. Call me on Monday March 11.

6. I am going to summer camp on Tuesday July 22 and he is going on vacation.

Notes for Home: Your child identified and placed commas in dates and in sentences with connecting words. **Home Activity:** Have your child show you his or her work on this page. Ask your child to explain why the commas are used where they are.

Read each sentence.
Add a comma where it belongs in each sentence.

1. Alisa wrote a story and she drew a picture.

2. Mom ran a race and we watched.

3. The students like to play outside but today it is raining.

4. My birthday is in March and I am having a party.

5. We lost our cat but she came home on her own.

Write three sentences about a family dinner.
Use and or **but** with a comma in each sentence.

6. _____
_____
_____

7. _____
_____
_____

8. _____
_____
_____

Notes for Home: Your child placed commas in sentences and wrote sentences, using commas.
Home Activity: Read a story with your child. Ask him or her to point out the commas and to explain why they are there.

© Scott Foresman 2

Circle the sentences that tell about the same idea. **Draw** a line through the sentence that does not tell about the same idea.

I like to play with my friends. We play games and sports.

Dogs can be small or big.

A **paragraph** is a group of sentences that tell about the same idea. The sentences are in an order that makes sense.

Circle the sentences that tell about the same idea.
Put these sentences in order to make a paragraph.
Write numbers in front of these sentences to show order.

_____ l. Other people keep stamps that are their favorite colors.

_____ 2. Many people collect stamps.

_____ 3. My brother likes to buy baseball cards.

_____ 4. Some people like stamps that show places.

_____ 5. Whatever their reasons are, people who collect stamps enjoy their hobby.

Notes for Home: Your child identified sentences that can be grouped into a paragraph. **Home Activity:** Look at a favorite story with your child. Have your child choose an interesting sentence or idea from the story, and help him or her write a paragraph about that sentence or idea.

Draw a box around the group of sentences that is in paragraph order. Write another sentence that fits in the paragraph.

1. Doug took the toy away from Rollo. Doug's dog Rollo broke a new toy car. Rollo put his head down on his paws.

2. Willa's mom got a new car. It was bright blue. Mom took Willa for a ride. Willa waved to the neighbors as they drove along.

_____

- -

_____

- -

_____

Number each sentence in paragraph order. **Draw** a line through the sentence that doesn't belong in the paragraph.

_____ Roxanne was waiting for her little sister Sue.

_____ Finally Roxanne saw her sister walking outside.

_____ Roxanne and her sister like to go swimming.

_____ First she saw her sister go into the library.

_____ Next Sue returned a book.

_____ Then the girls rode home on their bikes.

Notes for Home: Your child identified a paragraph and rearranged sentences in paragraph order. **Home Activity:** Talk with your child about what he or she did today. Then help your child write a paragraph to describe his or her day.